"Hope and praise in the midst of our darkest nights. Through their own struggles, Matt and Beth offer powerful and life-altering encouragement for us all."

Louie Giglio
Passion Conferences
Author, *I Am Not, but I Know I AM*

"I count it a great honor to call Matt and Beth my friends, and there are few people whom I respect more. This book is so timely and needed in the Church today. Every page seems to deal with what is left out of much of our worship. We all experience the bottom of life at some point, and interestingly, that's usually where we find God to be the closest and most familiar. Matt and Beth encourage us that in all things, the good and the bad, God is worthy of our praise."

Chris Tomlin
Songwriter and Worship Leader
Author, *The Way I Was Made*

"Matt and Beth's powerful anthem 'Blessed Be Your Name' is a gift to the Church; it has given us faith-filled words to declare when life seems to have crumbled around us. But Matt and Beth wouldn't have been able to write this song without enduring their own pain. In this book, they describe some of what they've suffered, and they share Scriptures that God used to console them. What a compassionate and mighty God we serve!"

Darlene Zschech
Songwriter and Worship Leader,
Hillsong Church, Sydney, Australia
Author, *Extravagant Worship* and *Kiss of Heaven*

D0167944

Finding God
in the Hard Times

Books by Matt and Beth Redman

Finding God in the Hard Times

*The Heart of Worship Files**

*Facedown**

*by Matt Redman

Finding God
in the Hard Times

Choosing to Trust and Hope
When You Can't See the Way

Matt and Beth Redman

BETHANYHOUSE
a division of Baker Publishing Group
Minneapolis, Minnesota

Published by Bethany House Publishers
11400 Hampshire Avenue South
Bloomington, Minnesota 55438
www.bethanyhouse.com

Bethany House Publishers is a division of
Baker Publishing Group, Grand Rapids, Michigan

Bethany House edition published 2016

ISBN 978-0-7642-1519-3

Previously published by Regal Books as *Blessed Be Your Name*, first edition 2005,
second edition 2008.

Printed in the United States of America

Library of Congress Control Number: 2016930526

Cover illustration by Wayne Brezinka
Cover design by Dan Pitts

16   17   18   19   20   21   22   7   6   5   4   3   2   1

Dedicated in loving memory of
Rachel McColl
and Natalie Kathryn Brown

Contents

Thanks to:

Don Williams and Louie Giglio
for support and feedback

Claire Prosser and Ellie Zaragoza
for lots of research and support

Jo Trevor for the statistics you provided

Pastor Jack Hayford and Pastor Andy Hickford
for your wise and powerful opening words

All at Bethany House/Baker Publishing Group

Foreword
to the First Edition

Stunned!

Shocked by circumstance!

Set back!

Shaken by life's earthquakes!

We've all gone through difficult times, but not all of us have managed them well—at least not when we were hit by the first of the many collisions that are a part of life. At some time, we will go through overwhelming and staggering events that will seem to shatter our life's horizon. These events come like lightning bolts—unpredictable and blinding—only to be inescapably followed by the rolling thunder of whatever aftermath the unwelcome eventuality brings.

Matt and Beth Redman have experienced such events and, as a result, not only have they given us a wonderful song to assist us in the face of such circumstances, but they also offer this book to encourage us. If you've "been there, done that" when it comes to having experienced trials that, while not shaking your faith, have left you shaken with questions, then you'll be blessed as Matt and Beth share these letters and their own stories of how in the midst of life's shattering moments, the Holy Spirit can bring us stability in the presence of the One who alone is able to calm our fears and address our questions with *himself*—the ultimate and only adequate Answer.

This song became an anchor to the life of our daughter Rebecca, as well as to the entire congregation at The Church On The Way, when Scott Bauer, Rebecca's husband, our son-in-law, and the congregation's senior pastor, died almost instantly at age forty-nine due to a massive hemorrhage from a brain aneurysm. In what we see as the prime of life, a beloved husband, father, and shepherd was suddenly transported to his eternal home. And while the confidence of his being "present with the Lord" held—and yes, *holds*—great spiritual comfort, derived from our faith in Jesus Christ, when such a shocking event occurs, seldom does immediate consolation come to the raw surfaces of our emotionality or the rough edges of our mind's reasoning.

God isn't offended by this. Indeed, Jesus' tears at Lazarus's tomb—even in the face of His knowing that He was about to raise Lazarus from the dead—are enough to assure us that He understands our grieving over life's losses, trials, or shaking circumstances. We *do* have a place of refuge in, and recourse to, the One who is "touched with the feeling" (Hebrews 4:15 KJV) of our weaknesses, pain, and struggles.

We, and our church family, tasted that compassion when Matt and Beth's God-given song became rich ministry to us and became a balm of healing in the congregation's life. Rebecca had called me the day after Scott died and said, "Dad, could we sing 'Blessed Be Your Name' on Sunday? I keep playing and singing it over and over here at home."

To my chagrin, I had to admit that I didn't know the song. Because Scott had assumed the oversight of the church, my travels had disallowed my keeping current with the congregation's worship repertoire. But I learned Matt and Beth's song that Sunday, and I can hardly describe the progressive infusion of faith it gave us—even more, *the joy beyond sorrow* that spread through all of us—during those first days after Scott's homegoing. We sang:

> And when the darkness closes in, Lord,
> Still I will say . . .
> Blessed be the name of the Lord,
> Blessed be Your glorious name.

Oh, what comfort! What a strong, stabilizing, comforting, dynamic, and Word-centered declaration!

And so, Matt and Beth, my deep thanks are extended to you. I understand, as composers do, that songs do not come without having paid a personal price to learn their truth. You have enriched us all by drawing us to the deep truth that, ultimately, knowing Jesus isn't about "getting blessed" or "receiving blessings." Rather, it's about knowing Him—the changelessly faithful One—no matter what is going on around us!

As you, dear reader, take up this book, I believe that you will be blessed and taken into the dimensions of enrichment that are only found in finding God's love and comfort *within trial and beyond sorrow.* Not only are God's love and comfort evident in the testimonies written in this book, but they are also timelessly and preciously promised in *His* Book: the solid, unshakable covenant of God's Word, which assures us,

> When you pass through the waters, I will be with you. . . .
> When you walk through the fire, you will not be burned
> (Isaiah 43:2).

Pastor Jack W. Hayford
Chancellor, The King's College and Seminary

Foreword
to the Second Edition

The phone rang at 5 a.m. Two dear friends were on the line. Their four-year-old was dying of a brain tumor and had been taken into the hospital—would I come and pray? For the next couple of hours, I just stood silently in the corner of the hospital room, pleading with God as two remarkable people tried to come to terms with every parent's worst nightmare as they comforted their young son in his last days.

Around 7 a.m., I got another call. This time it was Sarah, another church member, who was terminally ill with cancer. She had experienced a massive seizure that morning and had been rushed into the hospital. I went down to see her in the accident and emergency ward, and after she regained consciousness, we started chatting together. Sarah was a woman of great faith who knew that she was dying. We talked of our Christian hope of a new heaven and new earth, and agreed that one day we would like to "do" the coast of Donegal together! I treasure the memory of how keen she was to know whether I thought there would be Guinness available! She was still smiling when the hospice staff arrived to take her into their care.

All the while, however, I was anxious to make two phone calls of my own. The first was to Simon. The day before, he had technically died four times before being resuscitated. That morning, he was having life-saving heart surgery in Brighton. I wanted to pray with him before he went down to the operating room. I only just caught him in time. The second call was to my grandmother, who was in the hospital and very unwell. I really wanted to get to see her, but it was a three-hour drive and I needed to explain why it was not going to be possible that day.

Eventually at about 10 a.m., I got in the car and tried to go into the office. I didn't make it. I felt overwhelmed and emotionally exhausted. There was no way I was going to be able to concentrate. So I went to the beach, sat on the shore, and watched the waves come in.

Over the next three months, I was to bury three of those four people. Over the next three months, I was to sit on that beach many times.

What Matt and Beth have done in this beautiful book is to provide simple yet profound advice to help prepare Christians for those "beach moments." *Finding God in the Hard Times* provides the reader with the tools for lament—how to mourn in the presence of God. This book is, in effect, a framework of Christian thinking to help us filter and view life's pain. Of course, nothing can prepare us fully for suffering. Quick-fix remedies do not work and, I am glad to say, are not found in these pages. What is sensitively written here points us toward a God who longs to reveal himself in the worst of circumstances, a God who continues to bring victory in the face of death, a God who can still bring beauty out of the most awful and ugly things, a God in whom hope springs eternal.

Richard Wurmbrand, who himself was imprisoned and tortured for his faith, tried to explain it this way: "In prison we had to unlearn our theology and relearn *Theos*—God—the one of whom theology speaks. Nowhere in the Bible does it say that a Bible verse will comfort you. It's the living God of whom the Bible verse speaks who can only bring comfort in our suffering."

It is this God whom this book encourages us to meet in our pain. Blessed be His name!

Andy Hickford
Senior Minister, Maybridge Community Church
Worthing, England

Blessed Be Your Name

Blessed be Your name in the land that is plentiful,
Where Your streams of abundance flow,
Blessed be Your name.
And blessed be Your name when I'm found in the desert
    place,
Though I walk through the wilderness,
Blessed be Your name.

Every blessing You pour out I'll turn back to praise.
And when the darkness closes in, Lord,
Still I will say,

Blessed be the name of the Lord,
Blessed be Your name.
Blessed be the name of the Lord,
Blessed be Your glorious name.

Blessed be Your name when the sun's shining down
    on me,
When the world's "all as it should be,"
Blessed be Your name.
And blessed be Your name on the road marked with
    suffering,
Though there's pain in the offering,
Blessed be Your name.

Every blessing You pour out I'll turn back to praise,
And when the darkness closes in, Lord,
Still I will say,

Blessed be the name of the Lord,
Blessed be Your name.
Blessed be the name of the Lord,
Blessed be Your glorious name.

You give and take away,
You give and take away,
My heart will choose to say,
"Lord, blessed be Your name."

Matt and Beth Redman, © 2002 Thankyou Music/Adm. by
worshiptogether.com songs. Excl. U.K. & Europe, adm. by Kingsway
Music: tym@kingsway.co.uk. Used by permission.

Introduction

A few years ago, while on sabbatical, we found ourselves writing a little song called "Blessed Be Your Name." Wrapped around the themes of worship, suffering, and the sovereignty of God, the song was borne out of a deep conviction that, come pain or joy, to worship God is always the best decision to make. The song was the soundtrack to so much of our journey in God— fatherless times when He proved to be ever faithful, and seasons of rejection and abuse when God proved to be closer than we ever knew He was. By the grace of God, we'd seen enough to trust Him—no matter how dark things appeared to be. And trust gave birth to worship.

Since writing the song, we've heard so many stories of how the people of God have responded to Him in trust and praise—in some of the harshest life circumstances that we've ever come across. Letters, conversations, and emails have unveiled many different tales of abuse, rejection, and heartache— or stories of those who've lost loved ones in the most shocking of circumstances. Yet there's a common theme linking all of these reports together—a determined choice to press on with lives of praise amidst a world of pain. All of these worshipers have found themselves surrounded by the storms of life, and yet they have decided to respond to Jesus with a faithful cry of "Blessed be your name" in their hearts. Come rain or shine, come hardship or ease, come confusion or clarity, they are an army of worshipers making the daily choice to respond to God with an unshakable devotion. This book is for all those who long to be counted alongside this inspiring group of worshipers.

Matt and Beth Redman

God remains as faithful as the day He created you in love, and as powerful as the day He spoke the world into being.

one

My Heart
Will Choose to Say

Worship is always a choice. At times it's an easy, straightforward one. When life is peaceful and painless, the choice to respond to God in thanksgiving and praise may not be such a hard one to make. But at other times in our lives, worship becomes a much gutsier decision. Caught up amidst a whirlwind of pain and confusion, the decision to cry out, "Yet I will praise you!" is a costly act of devotion. In the life of every worshiper, there will come times when worship meets with suffering. And these moments shape what kind of worshipers we will become. Yes, praise be to God for times of abundance and plenty in our lives—those carefree days full of peace and laughter. Yet we praise Him also in the wilderness times—those dark and stormy seasons of the soul when we're left crying out with the psalmist, "How long, O LORD, how long?" (Psalm 6:3).

When trials come, trust must arise. When there's nothing to rock the boat, our trust in God is rarely tested. Seasons of stillness and calm are wonderful, yet before too long, the winds will start to gather, and we'll find ourselves caught up once again in the storms of life. The question then is this: Can we still find our way to the place of praise? We may have faith to believe in God as Lord of the *calm*—but do we also have faith to believe in Him as Lord of the *storm*? He is Lord of both the hurricane and the gentle breeze. The One who rules and reigns amidst all of the earthquakes of this life—those times when our whole world seems to be shaking and breaking apart.

For each of us, growing up was not an easy journey. Our childhood and teenage years were marked by family breakup and loss. Looking back now, our little stories are a testimony to the rescuing and restoring nature of God.

Matt Redman

For the first seven years of my life I was a carefree and contented little boy. All that changed one night in March 1981 when my dad died suddenly. It was a shocking time, and looking back now, I can still picture the moment I was told of his death. A few years later, I found out he'd actually committed suicide—which came as a bit of an aftershock, and brought with it some more painful questions. Was it anything to do with me? Did he not love us enough to stay around? But by the grace of God, this painful season propelled me toward Him, not away from Him.

A year or two later, my mum (herself a passionate fol-
lower of Christ) remarried—and at first it felt like I had a
new father. However, a couple of years in, things turned
sour, and we soon discovered that he wasn't the man of
integrity and faithfulness he claimed to be. After mistreat-
ing us as a family and abusing my trust, he was forced to
leave. And again we found ourselves "fatherless."

In these dark seasons of the soul, faith is either
strengthened or broken. Contentment and trust build
us up. Bitterness and complaint eat us up. History is full of
people who chose the path of bitterness and found themselves in an even worse place than where they started. But
wise worshipers know that the only healthy way ahead
is to take all they know of God and turn it into trust and
praise. By His grace, even in those early teenage years, I
had seen enough to know that God was good—and that
time would tell He was in control. Looking back now, I can
see His Father heart and His sovereign hand all over that
season of my life. The passage of time has demonstrated
what all along I knew to be true—that God is always
closer and kinder than we know; He is a father to the
fatherless.

Beth also had a grueling childhood, bullied and abused by
people she should have been able to trust. The key for both of
us was that we'd seen enough of Jesus to enable us to endure.
And while the enemy may have tried to use those bad circumstances to contradict the goodness of God in our minds and
hearts, by the grace of God, we'd encountered Him strongly
enough to trust Him—even in seasons when nothing seemed
to make sense.

Such times are like a case of spiritual car sickness. Motion sickness when you travel in a car is caused by your senses contradicting each other. Say, for example, you choose to read a book as you travel. The balance sensors in your ears tell you that you're moving quickly—yet your eyes report that you're not. It's a case of conflicting senses. One way to cure the sickness is to add more evidence to what you know to be correct. For example, rolling down the window and sticking your hand out of a fast-moving car will help confirm to your brain that you are indeed in motion.

The same is true of the spiritual life. There may come seasons of pain when we desperately try to cling to what we know to be true about God, and yet we are utterly confused by a hardship we're experiencing. Our knowledge of Scripture tells us that God is eternally good; yet at the same time, a very tough life situation seems to be screaming the complete opposite at us. Before long, we find ourselves in a case of spiritual motion sickness—living in the tension of what we think we know to be true, and the deep pain that seems to contradict it.

The key is to reinforce what deep down you know to be true, by adding extra revelation. Spiritually speaking, roll down the window and stick your hand out. Open the Bible and feed upon the truths of God and His faithfulness. Strengthen your understanding of His ways as you read. Find encouragement in the lives of those who chose to trust His power, grace, and purpose amidst their darkest hours. Look over His track record in your own life and in the lives of those you know to love Him.

See how often He has poured out the oil of kindness in times of trouble. How on many occasions He has rescued seemingly at the last possible moment—or turned around something that at the time seemed like it could never lead to fruitfulness. All of these things build faith in us. And faith will always fan the flames of worship.

The book of Lamentations gives us a great example of a worshiper who experienced pain and yet used the act of remembering as a pathway to praise. *The Message* words it like this:

> I remember it all . . . the feeling of hitting the bottom. But there's one other thing I remember, *and remembering, I keep a grip on hope.*
>
> Lamentations 3:20–21, emphasis added

What a fantastic way to give voice to this powerful principle! The discipline of remembering helps us keep a grip on hope and find our way on the paths of praise.

In the next verses of this chapter, the writer reminds his soul:

> GOD's loyal love couldn't have run out, his merciful love couldn't have dried up. They're created new every morning.
>
> Lamentations 3:22–23 THE MESSAGE

Returning to the car-sickness illustration, the worshiper here is consciously rolling down the window and sticking his hand out into the air that he might be affirmed and strengthened in what his heart, deep down, knows to be true about God.

The writer of Lamentations was not alone in his faith-building technique. The psalmists were constantly practicing this discipline. In so many of the psalms, the writer recalls the story of God's faithfulness as a bridge toward worship and hope. Psalm 13, for example, begins with a desperate cry but ends with a reminder of God's track record in his life:

> How long, O LORD? Will you forget me forever?
>   How long will you hide your face from me?
> How long must I wrestle with my thoughts
>   and day after day have sorrow in my heart?
> How long will my enemy triumph over me?
>
> vv. 1–2

Five urgent questions from a worshiper longing to be free of his suffering. Yet he ends his song with the choice to believe and trust in the powerful and merciful nature of his God:

> But I trust in your unfailing love;
>   my heart rejoices in your salvation.
> I will sing the LORD's praise,
>   for he has been good to me.
>
> Psalm 13:5–6

The psalmist here teaches us a beautiful truth: *Remembering releases rejoicing.*

Throughout the ages, the people of God have found strength in this approach. Take, for example, the writer of the old hymn "The Solid Rock"—a song deeply rooted in the truth of an unchangeable, unshakable Savior:

When darkness veils His lovely face,
I rest on His unchanging grace.[1]

In other words, in times when we can't seem to perceive God amidst our pain, and the clouds of anxiety and fear close in on us, the way forward is to remind ourselves of what we know to be true and dependable—the unchanging grace of God.

It's a little like looking at the moon. We've all seen a full moon and therefore know something of its form. But we don't always witness it like this. Some nights we see a half moon, at other times just a small sliver of moon. And on some occasions we see almost nothing at all—just the faintest outline hidden by a cloudy night sky. Yet the point is this: Even when the moon is obstructed from our view, we are still convinced of its existence and true form because of what we have seen in the past. The same is true of our walk as worshipers of Jesus. At times, painful life circumstances seem to obstruct our view of Him and His goodness. But we have seen the form of the Lord many times before—in life and in Scripture—and know Him to be as good and as kind as He ever was. Faced with challenging times, a wise worshiper looks over the form of the Lord—recalling the soul-refreshing wonders of His nature and attributes—and through this finds a way to the place of praise. Our Father in heaven has an incredible track record.

Faced with anguish and distress, the psalmist even talked to himself. To find strength and hope, he repeatedly speaks to his soul, reminding himself that there is One who can save him. Twice he cries out in Psalm 42:

Why, my soul, are you downcast?
  Why so disturbed within me?
Put your hope in God,
  for I will yet praise him,
  my Savior and my God.
  vv. 5–6, 11

If you yourself are in a season of struggle, take a moment now to remind yourself of the God who sees your struggle. It's possible to talk your soul into a place of hope. We worship a triumphant Savior, a victorious King. The all-powerful and all-loving God, who is faithful in all He says and gracious in all He does. The One who has never been anxious, overwhelmed, or outsmarted. The God of unbroken promises. When He acts, no one can reverse it. When He speaks, His commands never return empty. The God who never wastes His words. The doors He chooses to open, no one can close; and the doors He purposes to close, no one can open. No plan of His has ever been thwarted. No one has ever outmaneuvered Him, outlived Him, or out-loved Him. He remains as faithful as the day He created you in love, and as powerful as the day He spoke the world into being. And in your brokenness He stays as close and as involved as you want Him to be.

To worship God is to tell Him that we believe Him for who He says He is. Every day we're faced with the choice either to acknowledge and proclaim Him as the great and merciful God He declares himself to be or to deny Him. Intense though it may sound, the truth is this: If we deny something good about God, we automatically imply something bad about Him. If we deny God's sovereignty and power, we imply, to a degree at least, that He is weak and has lost control. If we can't bring ourselves to trust that He is full of mercy, then perhaps, at least in part, we're implying that He has a mean or uncaring streak. There is actually no middle ground. He is either the all-powerful, all-loving God His Word declares Him to be, or He is not.

That may sound a touch harsh. Please hear it in the context of the incredible wealth of patience, kindness, and compassion stored up for us in the heart of God. For in His amazing grace, our heavenly Father finds delight even in the most broken and fragile of our offerings—in the same way that an earthly father will rejoice upon receiving a simple yet heartfelt piece of art from his young child. Yet this is only one side of the mystery, for our God is also the majestic and holy King—worthy to be trusted and believed in for the wonderful truths He says about himself. He desires and requires faith, trust, and obedience—He wants worshipers who stake their lives on the truths of His nature and attributes.

Note the heart posture of a Nazi concentration camp prisoner who once scribbled these lines onto the wall of his cell:

> I believe in the sun,
> Even when it is not shining.
> I believe in love,
> Even when I feel it not.
> I believe in God,
> Even when He is silent.[2]

Yes, every act of worship is a choice—a decision to believe and respond to God for who He says He is—no matter how pressing our circumstances. And the greater the pain we're experiencing, the greater a choice it may be. Sometimes we will walk blindly, unable to understand why we are going through a certain situation—our only comfort being the knowledge that God himself is not walking blindly, but instead is wisely, kindly, and firmly in control. Indeed, as we will begin to see, so often our Father in heaven will take our broken moments and weave them into a powerful tapestry to the glory of His name.

Questions for Reflection

1. This chapter talks about the uneasiness we feel when bad circumstances conflict with our understanding of the goodness of God, calling this imbalance "spiritual car sickness." Write down several spiritual truths—perhaps verses you've memorized—that you can remind yourself of to reinforce what you know to be correct.

2. "Remembering releases rejoicing." Think back on some times in your past when God has revealed His goodness and love for you. Can you think of a way to keep these memories at the forefront of your mind when you're struggling with doubt and pain?

3. "Worship is a choice." Can you think of something you could do today to help you choose to worship, or as Matt and Beth put it, "Find your way to the place of praise"?

The church of God needs her songs of lament just as much as she needs her songs of victory.

two
_____

The Road Marked
With Suffering

On September 15, 2001, we flew into L.A. for the start of a sabbatical break in California. Four days earlier, we'd watched with the rest of the world, gripped by those terrible, nation-shaking events of 9/11. Over the next few days and weeks in the U.S., as we watched the news, talked with neighbors, and visited many different churches, the full effect of the terrorist attacks began to unfold before us. Brokenness was everywhere, and many people sought some kind of comfort in the church. Our landlady, who just weeks before had relocated to Manhattan, set foot inside a church building for the first time since her childhood. For the few weeks following those attacks, church attendance figures all over America went up dramatically.

During this time we had the privilege of visiting many different congregations. We were so inspired and impressed by the preachers. Virtually everywhere we went, pastors delivered biblical and powerful sermons, speaking into the pain of the nation. They eloquently and powerfully expressed the heart of God over a shocked and vulnerable people—and reminded them of His strength and sovereignty. But nearly everywhere we visited, a worrying question began to arise: Where were the songwriters at such a time as this? Where were the musical poets and prophets to help the people of God find a voice in worship at this tragic time? The truth was, in most places we visited (or led worship), there was a distinct lack of songs appropriate for this time. As songwriters and lead worshipers, we had a few expressions of hope at our disposal, but when it came to expressions of pain and lament, we had very little vocabulary to give voice to our heart cries. On a few occasions we did encounter a helpful song for these vulnerable times—but for the most part, it seemed as if we and many of our fellow lead worshipers were struggling to find the right tone. The truth is, the church of God needs her songs of lament just as much as she needs her songs of victory.

It wasn't the first time we'd noticed this gap. Once before, we'd flown into San Diego, California, for a worship conference—just a couple of days after a horrific school-shooting incident right there in the heart of the city. Since we were staying in town during one of the memorial services, we were asked to lead worship for some of the students and their families. We accepted straightaway and immediately began to ponder which songs might best fit the tone of the time. David Ruis's "Whom Have I But You?" was a godsend, and the hymn "Amazing Grace"—particularly the "dangers, toils, and snares" verse—played a big part too.[1] But again we were left in a slightly vacant space—struggling to find more songs that would help the community respond to God healthily, biblically, and honestly at such a time.

A few weeks after 9/11, we wrote the worship song "Blessed Be Your Name." It wasn't written consciously in response to those dark events—but no doubt, being immersed in the spiritual and emotional climate of those days was an important factor in birthing it. Many people ask if there was a particular life event that triggered the writing of this song, and in all truth, the answer is no. It's really a song borne out of the whole of life—a realization that we will all face seasons of pain or unease. And in these seasons we will need to find our voice before God. The church (and indeed the world) needs its songs of lament.

The people of God have always had their laments. The book of Psalms is filled with a host of intense emotions and expressions toward God. Many of the psalms were birthed in times of suffering and struggle. Psalm 3 was written as King David fled for his life from his own son, Absalom. Psalm 56 was inspired when the Philistines captured him in Gath. In Psalm 57, David is on the run again, this time from King Saul—and he wrote the song while hiding in a cave. These are songs formed in the fire of affliction. They are the desperate cries of a worshiper on the road marked with suffering. In fact, Eugene Peterson estimates that around 70 percent of the content of the book of Psalms is lament-based.[2]

Clearly, therefore, songs of lament are a very biblical theme to sing in worship. Yet they are also a relevant theme to sing—for we live in a world full of anguish and heartache. As Christians, yes, we live in victory—but paradoxically, we also exist as strangers in a foreign land, aching for home and knowing deep within us that the world we see before us is not as it should be. So the question is this: If songs of lament are, first, thoroughly biblical and, second, extremely relevant, then why on earth are there not more songs to help us voice these heart cries?

As Frederick W. Schmidt Jr. writes, these psalms do three things:

> They give us permission to ask our own questions about suffering. They model the capacity to ask questions we might otherwise suppress, but can never escape. And they model how those questions might be asked without fear of compromising our relationship with God or with other people.[3]

Not only do these songs help us to be "real" in worship—but as Mark Greene from the London Institute for Contemporary Christianity points out, they also help give us solidarity with the pain of the world.[4]

Some people may argue that lament is not an appropriate expression for gathered worship. They ask, "How can we respond in such a tone when not everyone in the room may be feeling that way?" Again, Mark Greene is helpful, pointing out that to think like that is far too individualistic.[5] Our gathered worship is a community event—and therefore we mourn with those who mourn and weep with those who weep. If we do not feel like lamenting on a particular occasion, then perhaps we can sing the song to identify with some in our church family (or indeed the world) who do. Maybe on another occasion they will be in a brighter place and yet will sing and cry out to God in solidarity with our pain. As Paul reminded us in 1 Corinthians 12:

> If one part suffers, every part suffers with it.
>
> v. 26

For those in pain, it's very freeing to realize that we may ask questions in worship. Jesus himself (our blueprint for perfect worship) did so as He suffered the agonies of the cross. The crucified King of kings uttered words from a psalm of lament as He hung in agony:

> My God, my God, why have you forsaken me?
>
> Psalm 22:1; Mark 15:34

Cries for help and painful questions are well within the bounds of healthy and biblical worship. The psalms model that for us on so many occasions. Yet what they also model is an underlying, worshipful trust in God. The cry of their writers, however loud or long, and however dark or desperate, never wanders into the realm of accusation. The psalmists never suggest that perhaps God is not who He says He is after all. And as Frederick Schmidt Jr. notes, the writers "strain and search for understanding and act on what they learn. But getting answers to their questions is not the basis of their relationship with God."[6]

Though they may be stripped of confidence, and though they may be struggling to muster up strength and faith, these worshipers never journey into utter *hopelessness*. Utter weakness and desperation, yes. Yet even in their most desperate of times, there is always an undercurrent of hope—a knowing conviction that though they walk through the valley of the shadow of death, their God is everything He says He is. He is both shepherd and fortress—the God of unequaled compassion and of unrivaled strength.

God delights in such offerings—an underlying trust in His goodness and greatness—when our circumstances around us seem to fly in the face of our beliefs. Perhaps in the same way that a seed of faith is enough to move a mighty mountain, so too a seed of hope and trust is enough to move the heart of almighty God.

Our good friend Tim Hughes wrote a powerful song that wraps itself around this theme of lament and questioning—yet is marked by an underlying sense of trust, which is never far below the surface. The searching cries of the verse allow us to be real before God, and confess in our brokenness that our lives are not as together as we would like them to be:

> I've had questions, without answers,
> I've known sorrow, I have known pain.

Yet next comes a brilliant flow of lyrics, reminding us of how a broken heart might move healthily onward in worship:

> When hope is lost, I'll call You Savior.
> When pain surrounds, I'll call You healer.[7]

When we're feeling abandoned or hopeless, we must declare Him as Savior. And when we're overcome by anguish and pain, we must throw ourselves at the feet of the One we know to be the healer. When our circumstances seem to dictate differently, the remedy is to confess, as urgently as possible, what deep down we know to be true about God.

It's important to note that in taking such a stand, we are not *bargaining* with God. It is not a case of "I'll scratch your back if you scratch mine"—or, in other words, "I'll call you Savior if you agree to heal me." Instead, we are proclaiming Him for who He is and then falling upon His mercy and good judgment. In His infinite wisdom and kindness, God may well purpose to bring us healing. But perhaps we will have to wait awhile to see our situation changed. Or perhaps we will never be healed this side of heaven. And if we are not, God hasn't become any less wise or merciful. Indeed, one day we may well realize for ourselves just how merciful and wise He was in withholding a healing. We are entirely in the hands of His great mercy and wisdom.

The story of Shadrach, Meshach, and Abednego in the book of Daniel demonstrates this attitude powerfully. Refusing to bow down in worship before anyone but their God, these worshipers are threatened with a raging furnace—certain death in the eyes of their aggressor and all those around them. Refusing to bow the knee in the face of repeated threats, they declare:

> If we are thrown into the blazing furnace, the God we serve is able to deliver us from it, and he will deliver us from Your Majesty's hand. *But even if he does not,* we want you to know, Your Majesty, that we will not serve your gods or worship the image of gold you have set up.
>
> Daniel 3:17–18, emphasis added

Of course, the story ends with their surviving the fire—without a hair on their head being singed and without even the smell of fire on them. But the real point here is that their attitude is a great role model for us as worshipers. In our darkest times, we must proclaim Jesus as the One who is powerful enough to heal and merciful enough to rescue. But all the time, underneath must be a conviction that even if for some reason we are not relieved of our struggle, our worship will not falter. At times, we may find ourselves faced with our own raging furnaces—be it persecution or other forms of suffering. And the principle is the same for us as it was for those friends of Daniel thousands of years ago. We rest worshipfully on a high view of the sovereignty of God and a deep knowledge of His Father heart.

At one time or another, we will all experience both sides of this situation—times when God grants our requests for healing or rescuing, and times when He chooses not to. At the time of writing, we're in the middle of a recent and still painful example of this, having just experienced a third successive miscarriage.

Beth Redman

When Matt and I suffered the loss of a baby again and again, I began to do what so many of us do when we're in pain—to notice how others around me were prosperous and blessed. How people who didn't even try to honor God seemed to have such fruitful lives without any hardship. I felt so dismayed and confused. It just seemed so upside down: to try to live right before God and aim to be humble and obedient, only to suffer as a consequence. Psalm 73 summed it all up for me:

> But as for me, I almost lost my footing.
>> My feet were slipping, and I was almost gone.
> For I envied the proud
>> when I saw them prosper. . . .
> They seem to live such a painless lives;
>> their bodies are so healthy and strong.
> They don't have troubles like other people;
>> they're not plagued with problems
>> like everyone else.
> Did I keep my heart pure for nothing?
>> Did I keep myself innocent for no reason?
>
> vv. 2–5, 13 NLT

To see the tiny frame of a baby's body, lifeless on a screen, with no heartbeat; and then, at an early stage of pregnancy, to have to go through a mini-labor and hand that baby back to Jesus—that was one of the hardest times in my life. Why was it happening? Then to lose two more babies in a row, even when I'd sought God so hard, was almost more than I could handle. Bitterness started to beckon, and again Psalm 73 seemed to perfectly describe my pain:

I must have seemed like a senseless animal to you.

v. 22 NLT

In the early stages of my first miscarriage, I hid away, battling in prayer. As I was physically losing the baby, I pleaded with God, for I knew He had the power to stop it. I became like Hannah in the temple, who pleaded and wailed for the baby she longed for. I knew that, in a moment, the baby could be restored and the pregnancy could continue. Would God show mercy and favor like He did to Hannah?

But there came a moment when I knew it was all over and that the baby was lost. From that moment on, I started to relate more to the story of King David—who himself lost a child after much prayer and petition (see 2 Samuel 12). David accepted the news of the child's death as the sovereign will of God, got up from the ground, and worshiped Him. There is a prayer that says, "God grant me the serenity to accept the things I cannot change," and that was the beauty of David's devotion in that moment. For there is a time to wail, weep, plead, shout, and grieve. But there is a time to accept the situation, get up off the floor, and somehow try to worship.

After our second miscarriage, I grieved harder and realized that the longing for a baby was all I could talk to God about. It almost had become an idol—with my desire for a baby starting to supersede my need and longing for God. I soon felt convicted—and once again found solace in the words of Psalm 73:

> Yet I still belong to you;
>   you are holding my right hand.
> You will keep on guiding me with your counsel,
>   leading me to a glorious destiny.

Whom have I in heaven but you?
I desire you more than anything on earth.
My health may fail, and my spirit may grow weak,
but God remains the strength of my heart;
he is mine forever.

vv. 23–26 NLT

By His grace I saw things in a new light—that even if I never had another baby, God had already given me everything I need in Christ Jesus.

Soon after our third miscarriage, we felt challenged with the words of 1 Thessalonians 5:16–18:

Rejoice always, pray continually, give thanks in all circumstances; for this is God's will for you in Christ Jesus.

In the midst of this turmoil it is right to grieve, and it is healthy to express our pain to God. But it is also God's will for us in Christ to be joyful, prayerful, and thankful in every circumstance. At times that is almost too hard for us—but if we can get hold of it, the deep and freeing truth is that if we're in Christ Jesus, we can never be completely joyless. As the apostle Paul described it, "Sorrowful, yet always rejoicing" (2 Corinthians 6:10). Yes, I still grieve—but in the depths of my heart I know that God himself is more than I need. And I know too that if it's His will for us to hold another baby in our arms, then no closed womb, no condition doctors cannot explain, no age barrier or genetic condition could ever hold back His plan.

A few years ago we discovered an old hymn by Laurence Tuttiett—a beautiful expression by a worshiper who had decided that come what may, he was determined to live for the glory of God:

> Father, let me dedicate all this [life] to thee,
> In whatever worldly state thou would have me be.
> Not from sorrow, pain, or care freedom dare I claim,
> This alone shall be my prayer, glorify thy Name.

It's a costly song to sing—for without a deep belief in God's sovereign wisdom and strength, and in His merciful and kind Father heart, it's far too risky a lyric to utter. The hymn continues along the same theme:

> Can a child presume to choose where or how to live?
> Can a Father's love refuse all the best to give? . . .
> Let my glad heart, while it sings, thee in all
>   proclaim,
> And, whate'er the future brings, glorify thy Name.[8]

This is a weighty offering of worship—standing before God, vowing to choose Him above the circumstances of this life, to love and follow Him come what may. But those who do so are never left disappointed, for you cannot out-give God.

There will no doubt be many things in this splintered world that we will not understand this side of heaven. And we simply take assurance in the fact that God is all we have, but more than we need. As John Piper writes:

> There are seasons of pain and loss and grief and darkness when nothing else is worth asking for but God.[9]

Questions for Reflection

1. This chapter talks about how mourning is not a typical theme of worship songs, and yet it's a common theme in the poetry of Scripture. Why do you think it's gone "out of style" in our age?

2. What does it mean, practically speaking, to "mourn with those who mourn"? Think about what you would want others to do for/with you when you're mourning, and then consider how you can fill that role in the lives of others who mourn.

So often, the soil of our suffering
will become the fertile ground for
our seasons of fruitfulness.

three

Though There's Pain
in the Offering

There's no doubt about it: This world is a harsh place to live. Every day, over two thousand people end their lives in suicide.[1] But no one goes through this world untouched by tragedy. All around us are people struggling to come to terms with suffering—so many stories of depression, rejection, terminal illness, miscarriage, bereavement, and many other hardships. On a wider scale, the picture can seem even bleaker. A daily glance at the evening news reminds us of what a harsh place we inhabit. Hardly a day goes by without a major tragedy hitting our screens. Floods and earthquakes, suicide bombers, train wrecks, pedophile networks, wars and famines, cancer scares—the list is seemingly endless.

Statistics provide us with yet more evidence of a broken world. In sub-Saharan Africa alone, some 25.4 million people are infected with HIV; in the year 2004 alone, an estimated 2.3 million people in that region died of full-blown AIDS. In fact, in nine African countries, life expectancy at birth has now dropped below forty years of age.[2]

If we're not careful, these news stories and statistics soon become just a list of facts and figures. But these reports are about real people—individuals struggling to retain the will to live as they carry their heavy burdens along the road of suffering. And the God of heaven, who has compassion on all that He has made, is weeping with them.

Wholesome worship never minimizes the pain of this world. It could be all too easy to sing our victorious songs, forever sweeping the hardships of this life under the carpet. A far healthier approach is to acknowledge before God the pain of this life, and then choose Him in the midst of it—not try to deny or somehow superficially rise above our pain, but instead welcome Him right into the reality of the situation. For some of us, worship will demand a gritty perseverance, by which we decide daily to choose the worth and ways of God over and above the pain of the struggle.

Yet wholesome worship, though not disregarding pain, does not disregard joy either. Even in the midst of deep pain, there is always an undercurrent of hope. For if we live in Christ, we can never be completely joyless. Yes, we must be honest and real in our struggles (as we've affirmed, lament is actively modeled in Scripture). But we must not sink down into the pit of despair and give up the fight, disregarding everything we know of God and disengaging with His merciful nature and goodness. If we do so, then we have lost our distinctiveness as followers of Christ, and our songs become no different from the despairing dirges of the culture around us—some of which start in pain, end in pain, and never have a hope of journeying anywhere else.

The Christian distinctive not only accepts pain as a fact of life but also learns to be thankful in it:

> Give thanks in all circumstances; for this is God's will for you in Christ Jesus.
>
> 1 Thessalonians 5:18

Though clearly we would never celebrate pain for pain's sake, from the canvas of Scripture and from the tapestry of our own lives, we begin to recognize that in times of anguish, God is always closer and more at work than we know. Though there is pain in the offering, we cry out, "Blessed be your name"— and before long, we often begin to witness the fruit of all He has accomplished in us or through us during these seasons of struggle. The writer of James expressed it like this:

> Consider it pure joy . . . whenever you face trials of many kinds, because you know that the testing of your faith develops perseverance. Let perseverance finish its work so that you may be mature and complete, not lacking anything.
>
> James 1:2–4

Journey through the New Testament, and we discover that time and time again the writers of these letters reinforce the same thread of teaching. First Peter 1:7 tells us that our temporary trials have come so that "the proven genuineness of your faith—of greater worth than gold, which perishes even though refined by fire—may result in praise, glory and honor when Jesus Christ is revealed." The apostle Paul did not unwillingly endure hardships, but for the sake of Christ, delighted in them—for he knew a deep truth:

When I am weak, then I am strong.

2 Corinthians 12:10

The book of Hebrews encourages us to see hardship as discipline—reasoning that it's all part of being a child of God:

Endure hardship as discipline; God is treating you as his children. For what children are not disciplined by their father? If you are not disciplined—and everyone undergoes discipline—then you are not legitimate, not true sons and daughters at all.

12:7–8

The writer continues on:

They disciplined us for a while as they thought best; but God disciplines us for our good, in order that we may share in his holiness. No discipline seems pleasant at the time, but painful. Later on, however, it produces a harvest of righteousness and peace for those who have been trained by it.

12:10–11

These two verses are vital to our understanding of this whole process in God. The writer makes it clear that it's not a case of masochism; in other words, we don't enjoy being in pain. No discipline seems pleasant at the time. In our hearts, minds, or bodies, we may be struggling beneath the pain of a testing situation. But deep in our spirits, we learn to consider it joy, knowing that we not only can find Christ in the situation but also can become more like Him as a result of it. There are no wasted seasons in the economy of God.

In *The Message*, Eugene Peterson phrases this Hebrews passage beautifully, throwing yet more light on the essence of the passage:

> My dear child, don't shrug off God's discipline,
>   but don't be crushed by it either.
> It's the child he loves that he disciplines;
>   the child he embraces, he also corrects.
>
> Hebrews 12:5–6

As C. S. Lewis once wrote:

> God whispers to us in our pleasures, speaks in our conscience, but shouts in our pains—it is his megaphone to rouse a deaf world.[3]

The more we journey through these New Testament letters, the more we recognize just how prominent this thread of teaching is. In 2 Corinthians 1:8–9, Paul recognizes that he suffered so that he might become more dependent on God. And the apostle Peter tells his readers that grief and trials have come so that their faith can be proved genuine and can result in "praise, glory and honor" (1 Peter 1:7).

Hebrews 2:10 tells us that Jesus himself was made "perfect through what he suffered." Or as the New Living Translation expresses it, "And it was only right that he should make Jesus, through his suffering, a perfect leader, fit to bring them into their salvation." To see this throws a whole new light on our thinking about the trials of this life. If we are seeking to be followers of Jesus, sharpened and matured in our faith, can we really expect to escape times of suffering, when the Author and Perfecter of our faith embraced and endured them?

This area is in many ways a hard teaching, and if it wasn't in the Bible in such clear and blunt language, we might even find it hard to swallow. The truth is, so often when we perceive God to have left us to struggle alone, the complete opposite is in fact true—He has not left the scene, but instead is doing a deep work in us. C. S. Lewis helps us further understand this biblical way of thinking:

> We are . . . a Divine work of art, something that God is making, and therefore something with which He will not be satisfied until it has a certain character. Over a sketch made idly to amuse a child, an artist may not take much trouble: he may be content to let it go even though it is not exactly as he meant it to be. But over the great picture of his life—the work which he loves . . . he will take endless trouble—and would, doubtless, thereby give endless trouble to the picture. . . . One can imagine a picture, after being rubbed and scraped and recommenced for the tenth time, wishing that it were only a thumbnail sketch whose making was over in a minute. In the same way, it is natural for us to

wish that God had designed for us a less glorious and less arduous destiny; but then we are wishing not for more love but for less.[4]

What an amazing insight into this process! We are back to Hebrews 12—that those whom our heavenly Father loves, He disciplines. His hand may be heavy upon us at times, yet He comes to discipline, not to condemn. "There is now no condemnation for those who are in Christ Jesus" (Romans 8:1).

Though the discipline may not seem pleasant at the time, it's far easier to endure (or count as joy and delight in!) if somehow within the bigger picture we manage to see the brushstrokes of God. As the seventeenth-century Madame Guyon commented:

> It is the fire of suffering which will bring forth the gold of godliness.[5]

A word of warning: We're not trying to advocate that every kind of suffering is merely a blessing in disguise. That could be a massively insensitive stance to take, especially in the light of major world tragedies, such as Auschwitz or the relatively more recent South Asian tsunami. Or even in light of something far more individual and personal, such as losing a loved one. We can't simply tidy away the issue of suffering into an "every cloud has a silver lining" drawer. The issue is far more complex than that—and many times we ourselves cannot provide a satisfactory answer to the question of why suffering occurs. To always attempt an explanation may at times put us at risk of belittling someone's experience of suffering—or in danger of second-guessing almighty God. As Frederick Schmidt Jr. writes, "It would be arrogant or irreverent for us to claim we completely understand the mind of God."[6] Some situations are far beyond our fathoming. And whether or not we can directly trace the handiwork of God in a certain situation, we can always find comfort in the fact that He is closer than we know. God is not in the habit of leaving us stranded.

And yet, so often we do begin to see God at work even in the hardest of circumstances. The story of Joseph in the book of Genesis provides us with an inspiring example of this. Toward the end of the story, after Joseph had been beaten up by his brothers and sold into slavery, and then elevated in Pharaoh's court, only to be imprisoned unjustly once again, he explains to his repentant brothers his take on things:

> You intended to harm me, but God intended it for good.
>
> Genesis 50:20

Joseph goes on to explain that God used the situation to bring about the saving of many lives. We would do well to follow Joseph and adopt a heart posture that is quick to recognize the hand of the Lord working even in times of trouble. Years before this, Joseph had learned this dynamic of God's working in the midst of suffering:

> The second son [Joseph] named Ephraim and said, "It is because God has made me fruitful in the land of my suffering."
>
> Genesis 41:52

This is a vital principle to keep hold of if we're to persevere. So often the soil of our suffering will become the fertile ground for our seasons of fruitfulness. The sooner we recognize this principle at work in various situations, the less painful they may be. If we can see that we will reap a harvest, we will have a greater readiness to sow in tears.

We've experienced this in our lives—so many of the hardest times have led to fruitfulness in our own lives and in the kingdom. What was meant for harm, God meant for good, bringing beauty out of ashes and making us fruitful in the land of our suffering. It's now clear to see how, during years of rejection and abuse early on in our lives, God drew us close to himself and turned those years around to prepare us for lives of kingdom ministry in Him.

Throughout the Bible we see this pattern time and time again. Just as God did in the life of Joseph, in His wisdom He often puts His people through a training school to prepare them for work in His kingdom. King David is a prime example. Anointed for victory in his battle against Goliath, David soon became a national hero, and his profile accelerated rapidly. People began to sing their songs about him, and he enjoyed favor in the courts of the king, where he then lived. Humanly speaking, he may have been thinking, *Now is my time.* He knew full well that he'd been anointed as the next king— and surely that was the logical next step, wasn't it? But things soon turned sour, and God propelled him into a season of yet more character training—living in caves for seven years, while the bitter King Saul sought to kill him. In that season he must have asked what on earth was happening—it seemed as if the call on His life was slipping through his fingers. But God had other plans: He used this time in the desert as an opportunity to form in David the qualities He required for a king. David was soon to be trusted with an incredible amount of fame, fortune, and power—and this season of hardship would sharpen him as the next leader of God's people. Suffering prepared him for the entrustment of kingship.

In John 15, Jesus paints a fantastic picture of how God often works in our lives. He describes the Father as a gardener, telling His disciples:

> He cuts off every branch in me that bears no fruit, while every branch that does bear fruit he prunes so that it will be even more fruitful.

v. 2

In the natural world, the pruning of a rose bush, for example, ensures that excess is removed, and helps to concentrate energy in the plant—getting it ready for more fruitfulness. In the same way, God gets involved in our lives, pruning even what is fruitful so that we may blossom more in our walk with Him.

Matt Redman

Seven years ago, I experienced a very real sense of God's pruning when I developed an acute form of tendonitis in my arm. In that particular season, I was crazily busy as a lead worshiper, leading worship at church, recording an album, and traveling at the same time—with little rest in between. It all came to a head one weekend when, after four days of nonstop guitar-playing in the studio, I headed off to Holland for some worship gatherings. On Friday night, I started to feel a strong twinge in my strumming arm, which by Saturday had turned into an agonizing pain. By Sunday morning, I could barely move my whole arm and hand. Seeking medical advice for nearly a week, and misdiagnosed on more than one occasion, I finally found a specialist, who informed me that my hand had frozen up. He then told me that if I'd come a day or two later, I would perhaps have lost full use of that hand. It was a scary moment.

I couldn't play guitar for seven weeks, and during that time many people prayed for me and sent encouraging words. Most of the words hit the mark powerfully, and their insights resonated deep within me. One or two, though, focused intensely on the phrase "the work of the enemy." Strangely, these didn't sit well with me—for by then I had a strong conviction that enemy or no enemy, what I was experiencing, more than anything else in that season, was a deep work of the Lord in me. As a lead worshiper, I'd become far too busy—and busyness had led me to neglect some of the main and plain things of the Christian walk, such as being mindful of the Lord in prayer and through His Word. This painful time was a spiritual pit stop—a chance to have some vital work done under the hood before any lasting damage occurred. God was reminding me that the *work of the Lord* should never outweigh the *Lord of the work*—and that I was a *son* long before I was a *servant*. Stripping me of pride and self-confidence also, my Father was reminding me that His power is made perfect in weakness.

To this day I don't know exactly what was at play theologically during that time. Was it the Lord inflicting it?

Or was it the Lord allowing the enemy to do so? These questions slowly faded into the background, as I rested safe in the knowledge that, whatever the case, my Father was very much in control, disciplining me with kindness and care—in the way that a perfect Father does.

When we look back over our lives, we can see the Lord's marks of kindness everywhere. So often in times of joy and celebration, all of us are quick to recognize the hand of God. But as mature Christians we begin to recognize His presence in the face of adversity too—seeing God powerfully at work in our brokenness.

Recently we were out driving in the countryside when we suddenly realized that we were nearly out of fuel. From that moment on, the journey changed. We were as light on the gas pedal as possible, driving carefully at an optimum speed for efficiency, and staring hopefully out the window for the first sign of a place to refuel. We had realized our emptiness, recognizing afresh just how dependent on fuel we were—and becoming much more thankful for every drop, treating it as something precious.

The same dynamic happens in the life of every worshiper. We may go through life cruising comfortably, taking the things of God for granted, and therefore not as mindful of Him as we should be. It's in these times that in God's great mercy, He shakes us up to realize our dependence on Him and our brokenness without Him. He may strip us of something we have come to depend on outside of Him, or find another way to remind us of our poverty without Him. Before long, there's a new sense of dependence on Him, and a heightened gratitude for every single drop of His grace in our lives.

Sometimes, on this journey, it may take months—even years—for the full evidence of fruitfulness to appear before our eyes. Such seasons require endurance and patience, and they challenge us to leave behind our "instant everything" mentality, which is so prominent in today's culture. When it comes to the kingdom of God, fast food spirituality is not on the menu. We're left instead to embrace these seasons of silence, once again leaning upon the track record of God's faithfulness, until rejoicing arrives in the morning. As Oswald Chambers both challenges and encourages us:

> Has God trusted you with a silence—a silence that is big with meaning? . . . If God has given you a silence, praise Him, He is bringing you into the great run of His purposes.[7]

There may be a time of waiting—and then all at once it becomes very evident that God has made us fruitful in the land of our suffering. Yet, as we acknowledged previously, for all of us there will be times when however hard we scrutinize the situation, however much we search for wisdom from Scripture or seek counsel from a pastor, we simply cannot begin to understand where God is in our suffering. And this will always be a much harder pill to swallow. There are situations on this earth that we may never fully make sense of while we're living here—taking comfort only in the fact that we are not alone in our suffering. God himself is involved—weeping with those who weep and drawing near to the brokenhearted. The wonderful truth is that, however broken we feel, we have not been left alone to make our own way out of the darkness. Even though we walk through the shadow of death, we learn to recognize the closeness of Jesus—for shadows can only be caused by the presence of light.

And here and now upon the earth, the cross of Christ illuminates our way on the road marked with suffering. In the light of Calvary, where the Son of God so willingly surrendered His life for this world, we find both strength and hope for our times of need. The cross reminds us that we worship a God who identifies with our suffering. One who is able to show both compassion and empathy, for He himself was overwhelmed by anguish and pain. Yet the cross also works another miracle—wherein the mercy of that place begins to outweigh the misery of our situation. Somewhere deep within we may still be asking, "Jesus, why am I suffering in this way?" But before long, that question, valid as it may be, will be superseded by another. Standing at the foot of the cross, we begin to ask, "Jesus, how can it be that you would suffer in that way?" The answer reminds us that we are not alone in suffering; more than anything, it assures us once again of the magnitude of His mercy. It is not escapism, but realism. The mercy of God outweighs the mess of our lives.

Questions for Reflection

1. First Thessalonians 5:18 tells us, "Give thanks in all circumstances; for this is God's will for you in Christ Jesus." What could you thank God for in the darkest moment

you've faced in your life—whether now or in the past? Express that gratitude to Him now.

2. This chapter talks about trials being used to make us all God wants us to be. How is God using trials in your life right now to change you for the better?

3. At one point Matt and Beth talk about discipline as "the Lord's marks of kindness." Sometimes it takes many years to see the payoff. Can you think of an event or circumstance in your life that produced fruit, but only after a long waiting period?

Every day God is working out
His wonders all around us.

four

Turn It Back to Praise

So far in the pages of this book we've looked at worshiping God on the road marked with suffering. But let's focus for one chapter on the other side of things—making sure that we journey to the place of praise in times of abundance. The fact is, we can be quick to question God when things go wrong for us, but slow to honor Him when things go well. The challenge is to take every blessing He pours out on our lives and turn it back into praise. As someone once commented, "Saying thank you is more than good manners. It is good spirituality."[1]

Gratitude is an essential ingredient in our worship "diet." Indeed, thanksgiving has always been a great way for the people of God to take a first step into worship. As Psalm 100 exhorts us,

Enter his gates with thanksgiving
and his courts with praise;
give thanks to him and praise his name.

vv. 4–5

Gratitude is a heart attitude that we must train ourselves in—for we're so quick to neglect it. Scanning through Scripture, time and again we see the people of God needing some direction in this area. The story of the Exodus and the people of God wandering discontentedly around the desert show just how easy it is for murmuring and moaning to set in—leading us far from the paths of gratitude and contentment. And on many occasions, the likes of the Psalms and the New Testament letters remind us to be thankful—highlighting yet again that this may not always be the first instinct of our hearts. The story of the ten lepers illuminates this even further. Jesus healed all ten, but only one returned to Him in thanks and praise (see Luke 17:11–37). Where were the other nine? For some reason, they just kept on walking. Perhaps they had meant to return in thanksgiving at some point but became distracted with celebrating and never quite got around to it. Perhaps they got too wrapped up in themselves and forgot the One who was the source of their joy and healing. Yet it's easy to see ourselves in this picture—so often receiving the gift, but somehow, in the midst of the blessing, forgetting the Giver. Our consumer-driven society has birthed a generation of takers. We'd do well to be led in worship by that one returning leper—who praised God loudly and threw himself at the feet of Jesus in extravagant thanksgiving.

The discipline of thanksgiving involves a constant stream of decisions to recognize and respond to the many kindnesses that have been poured out on us. The more we cultivate this heart posture, the more it will begin to flow naturally in our lives. It's like a small snowball at the top of a hill. Choose to set it in motion, guiding it down the slope, and it soon grows larger and larger. At a certain point, it runs away with itself, developing a momentum all its own. In the same way, when we become mindful of thanking God for even the smallest details of our lives, we soon find ourselves caught up in an endless list of things to be grateful for.

We need look no further than our bodies to get the ball rolling. The biology of our bodies has to be one of the most overlooked things when it comes to prayers of gratitude toward God. Do you like your own body? You should. We are an incredible mix of cells—with organs of such mind-blowing complexity that the best man-made technologies of our day still come no where near matching them. So many of the complex internal parts we use every day, we barely give a second thought to. But when we take a moment to marvel at them, they become a fantastic opportunity to explode in thankfulness before God.

Take the brain, for example. When was the last time you thanked God for your brain? That you can remember names, faces, and life events? That you can read the pages of His Word and store Scripture verses in your mind? That you can compute, conceive, and store in your memory so many of the wonders He has made? With 500,000 kilometers of nerve fibers, and messages traveling along them at speeds of a hurricane-force wind, the brain is something to be incredibly thankful for.[2] Yet it is just one part of our fantastically designed anatomy.

When was the last time you went to God in gratitude for your heart? The human heart beats 100,000 times a day and, in the space of seventy years, would pump enough blood to fill a skyscraper. The volume of blood pumped each minute is about five liters. But during physical exertion, the volume per minute can rise to twenty-five liters—so that the entire blood volume is pumped through the body five times per minute.[3] You'll never give thanks with a grateful heart in the same way again!

Move on to your senses—have you ever wondered that you can smell your favorite flower, taste your favorite food, and hear all kinds of interesting and moving music? And have you ever thought of giving thanks for something as seemingly ordinary as your skin? If not, then now might be a good time. One square centimeter of your skin contains about 6 million cells, 100 sweat glands, and 5,000 sensory corpuscles—as well as 200 pain points, 25 pressure points, 12 cold-sensitive points and 2 heat-sensitive points.[4] We take for granted this amazing part of our created bodies—but when we begin to investigate it, we are led through the gates of thanksgiving into the courts of praise. We join with the psalmist in crying out:

> I praise you because I am fearfully and
>   wonderfully made;
>   your works are wonderful,
>   I know that full well.

> Psalm 139:14

Next, move on to your family and friends. Think about your social circles—how God has skillfully woven them together, bringing people into your world for whom you will be ever grateful. For those with the eyes to see, the depths of His providence are swirling all around us. As a personal example, we've been married for seven years—and looking back, we're so appreciative of the depths of God's providence at work in our relationship. We first set eyes upon each other in a church parking lot in England. What a romantic, yet holy, setting! We praise God for that brief moment—that in His beautiful way He would let our paths cross for a short while, smiling upon the long-term plan He had to knit our lives together. Over the years, though we were living three hours apart, a strong friendship started to grow; a while later we were working together on the staff of a church. In the end, it took a runaway mouse in the church building to bring us together. (It's a long story, but you'd be surprised what two hours of trying to catch a mouse together can do for a relationship!) The point is this: We must learn to rehearse the stories of God's providence in our lives—thanking Him for both the smallest details and the grandest designs. Every day God is working out His wonders all around us.

If we can begin to take regular, small steps into thankfulness, then before long we will pick up our pace and find ourselves taking great big strides of praise. Too often we neglect even the small things—for instance, saying grace before a meal. In one way, this is a small thing. Yet if we begin to adopt this discipline, we begin to carve out space two or three times each day to thank God for His provision. The arrival of the food on our table gives many reasons to be thankful. To illustrate this, let's consider the vegetables we eat. On the journey between the soil and our plates, they have been grown, harvested, cleaned, transported, sold, and cooked. We thank God for their provision, but we must also thank Him for the many hands that have labored to bring them to us.

Before long, we're on to big steps in thanksgiving—thanking God for some of the grand themes of the Christian life. The writer of Psalm 103 exhorts us:

> Praise the LORD, my soul,
>> and forget not all his benefits—
> who forgives all your sins
>> and heals all your diseases,
> who redeems your life from the pit
>> and crowns you with love and compassion,
> who satisfies your desires with good things
>> so that your youth is renewed like the eagle's.
>
> vv. 2–5

Salvation, healing, forgiveness, compassion, and renewal—these are themes we should visit every day of our walk with God, and each of them can be found at the place of the cross. The hymn writer Fanny Crosby wrote, "Keep me near the cross," which is a great heart cry for any worshiper.[5] For when we stop going by the cross, we begin to lose sight of the depths of the pit we've been rescued from—and the heights of the mercy that saved us.

A thankful heart may not come easily—we can be so quick to let something not going so well in our lives cloud over the multitude of little blessings we have to be grateful for. Or else we spend hours asking God for something, yet only minutes thanking Him when He answers our prayers. Another pitfall in worship is to spend lots of time telling God what we have done for Him and neglect to thank Him for the far more momentous scope of what He has done for us. In all of these areas, we must ask the Holy Spirit to help us cultivate a lifestyle and a mindset of gratitude.

Another way to start out along this road is to thank Him as the God of yesterday, today, and forever—the One who was and is and is to come. In other words, begin by recalling a wonder He has worked somewhere along your life's journey. Walk through your testimony in your heart and mind; go again by the place of the cross and see all that He has won for you and done for you in that momentous place. Move on to the empty tomb and dwell for a moment on the joy of sharing in His resurrection. This is the first stage—thanking Him as the *God of yesterday.*

Next, bring gratitude for a kindness that He's worked in your life today—perhaps an answered prayer or a friendship you value. This is to worship Him as the *God of today.* And last, look to the horizon and thank Him in advance for a wonder still to come, praising Him as the *God of forever* and thanking Him for the life that is to come. This kind of model frees us up from a mentality of grumbling and trains us in the way of gratitude. We join with the hymn "Great Is Thy Faithfulness," reminding ourselves of God's consistent love and care for us in days gone by and worshiping Him as the bringer of "strength for today and bright hope for tomorrow."[6]

Mature worshipers of Jesus learn to bring an offering in every season of the soul, for every high and every low, knowing that the worth of Jesus outweighs each and every pain and pleasure in this life. Centered on Christ, wholesome worship has room both for the heights of joy and the pits of despair. Every blessing He pours out, we turn back to praise. And even when the dark times close in on us, still we will be singing out, "Blessed be your name."

Questions for Reflection

1. This chapter refers to thanksgiving as a discipline. Think of new ways you could implement this discipline into your daily life. What are some things you could do to remind yourself to have this mindset?

2. Matt and Beth mention some categories of things in our lives to be grateful for—our bodies, family, friends, our salvation. What are some other categories they didn't mention that you can add to this list?

3. We can also thank God for what He will do in the future. What are some scriptural promises that we can trust in, and thank God in advance for fulfilling?

Oh, that God would bring us to the place
that even when the familiar and the comfortable fall away beneath us, still we are
found with an undying song of trust flowing
from our lips and from our lives.

five

You Give and Take Away

The last section of the song "Blessed Be Your Name" comes straight from the story of Job. In what has to be one of the most intense stories in the whole of Scripture, Job is stripped of everything precious to him and suffers much hardship. Toward the beginning of his ordeal, he finds a way to the place of praise, falling to the ground in worship and crying out:

> The LORD gave and the LORD has taken away. Blessed be the name of the LORD.
>
> Job 1:21 NASB

This resounding line is a challenge for every worshiper. A call to trust deeply in the sovereignty of God, shaping our lives based not on the temporary things of the earth but on the eternal King of heaven. For devotion to stand the test of time and endure through every season of the soul, it cannot be based on the ever-changing circumstances of our lives—it must have its foundation on the never-changing worth of God.

In 1744, the hymn writer Charles Wesley was leading a worship gathering in an upstairs room in the city of Leeds, England. The meeting room was crammed full—when all of a sudden, the floor gave way, with all one hundred people falling into the room below! Wesley's reaction to this situation was inspiring. Seeing first that no one was seriously injured, he began to sing the doxology: "Praise God from whom all blessings flow." Not only that, but afterward he composed several hymns based on this event—using the broken floor as a picture of the uncertain things of this world, and contrasting it with the unshakable nature of God, His kingdom, and His Word.

The question for us is this: What do we do when our world falls in? What shape does our worship take when things that we depend on give way beneath us? Can we, as Wesley, be found with an unswerving song of worship on our lips? Oh, that God would bring us to that place—that even when the familiar and the comfortable fall away beneath us, still we are found with an undying song of trust flowing from our lips and from our lives.

There may actually be times when trust is just about all we can bring as an offering to God. Times of pain and struggle, when we've come to the end of ourselves and feel like we have nothing left to give. In these moments, to say to God, "I trust you," can be an offering pleasing enough in and of itself. We trust that God cares for us with a deep fatherly affection. We trust that His arm is never too short to save. We trust that He hears those who call upon His name. We trust that He is high enough to see things that we could never see. We trust that He is quick to show compassion, slow to anger, and abounding in love. In all of these offerings, we are telling God that despite our circumstances, we still believe He is who He says He is. And God loves that kind of heart response.

As we mentioned in the introduction, since writing the song "Blessed Be Your Name," we've had the privilege of hearing so many testimonies of how worshipers have found a way to endure even in the harshest of life's circumstances. Many of these testimonies have been beautiful and profound.[1]

◇◇

Dunblane, Perthshire
19 June 2003

Dear Matt and Beth,

Our precious youngest daughter, Rachel, died on 25th February this year. She was four years old. We have four other children: two girls—Brodie, eighteen, and Maggie, seventeen; and two boys—Harry, ten, and William, eight. Rachel was a beautiful gift loved by us more than I can begin to describe.

She was a totally healthy child until she took chicken pox in December 2002. It turned into pneumonitis, a rare complication, and she was rushed to intensive care in the Edinburgh kids hospital, where she was on life support for nearly three weeks. She was very sick but made a wonderful recovery—delighting the doctors and nurses.

We brought her home on Christmas Eve, and although Rachel was very weak, we managed. It will always be our most memorable

Christmas. She regained strength gradually and started to walk again after a few weeks, returning to her school nursery—full of joy in her recovery and very aware of how loved and special she was.

Then she became suddenly ill through the night of 24 February, and I rushed her to Stirling Royal Infirmary. She had developed septicaemia, which led to heart failure—and she died within four hours of reaching hospital. It is still hard for me to believe, however often I have painfully relived the events of that day.

We are all Christians, and when we were thinking of Rachel's funeral, we all knew immediately that we wanted the song "Blessed Be Your Name" in the service. It had been sung in our church and was prominent when Rachel and I were in hospital, but it took on a strong significance for us after her death. The words gave us strength and said what we wanted to say.

There were about 400 people in Dunblane Cathedral for the funeral. Our pastor took the service, and God gave us the strength we prayed for. The band led "Blessed Be Your Name." It was beautiful, powerful, and moving—and our family sang from our hearts.

Rachel will always be a part of us, and as time passes, it means such a lot when others remember her. We are missing her so much. The many tears I have shed while writing this letter have been strangely comforting amidst the pain. I have struggled very often to praise God since Rachel's funeral, but He does not let me go; and in the darkness, the only light and hope come from Christ, whose loving arms hold my darling Rachel.

With love,
Ruth McColl

◇◇◇◇◇◇◇

Columbus, Ohio, U.S.A.
4 April 2005

Dear Matt and Beth,

We lost our eighteen-year-old daughter, Natalie, two years ago, in an auto accident. It was her last day of high school. Ten short days before her high school graduation. She was the light of our lives. My love for Jesus has helped me through some of my darkest times. When I became an active Christian, the only thing I ever asked of God was to please not test my love for Him through Natalie. I prayed that every day for eight years. At the hospital, I kept telling all the pastors, "But this was the only thing I have ever truly asked of God."

It took me a few months to start attending church again. I wasn't mad at Him—I was hurt, confused, and even scared of Him. It was and is so bittersweet. We prayed and prayed for a miracle that day. We watched all her young friends, sitting in the waiting room in prayer circles and asking for that miracle, but it was not to be.

To attend church services and sing praise to Him about all the miracles He has performed and about what a loving God He is, and to not have my Natalie sitting next to me was so very hard.

Then we heard your song, and to us it just fit our situation so well that we now call it Natalie's song. Jeff and I always end up in tears when we get to the part about "He gives and takes away." That is so true. As a Christian, I understand that we are all God's children, big and small, young and old; but as a mother, she was my little girl. It is so hard to let go of her.

She was a hero to the end. She was an organ donor and saved four lives. She was always our "little special," but now she is to many, many more.

Blessings to you and your family.
With God's love,
Kathy Sayre

◇◇

These worship-filled letters were written by worshipers who did not deny the pain of their loss, but stood in the midst of it, choosing to trust God. Heaven knows they have made a good choice.

Our pastor recently commented that Christ-centered funerals are some of the best showcases for Christianity. That for those who trust their lives to Jesus, there is a wonderful distinctiveness when it comes to marking loss. Outside of Christ, many a memorial service or funeral is a groping in the dark—a heavy cloud of grief with no clarity as to what lies beyond it. There may be a meaningful celebration of a person's days on the earth, but without a Christ-centered hope, this will always be outweighed by the lack of confidence in a life everlasting. When the world only brings a vocabulary of sorrow and loss, in contrast the memorial service of a worshiper of Jesus is infused with a deep sense of thankfulness and hope. Yes, there is still the pain of loss, but it's outweighed by what we know to be true of God and of His promises for those who love Him. Only those who are rooted in such a faith can dare to say, "The Lord gives and the Lord takes away. Blessed be the name of the Lord." Without a deep knowledge of the Father heart of God and a faith in His sovereign power and wisdom, it's far too dangerous a thing to pray.

One man who adopted this heart stance was the eighteenth-century English poet and hymn writer William Cowper. One of his most well-known hymns is an amazing poetic and biblical response that comes from a man surrendered to the sovereignty of God:

> God moves in a mysterious way,
> His wonders to perform;
> He plants His footsteps in the sea
> And rides upon the storm.
>
> Deep in unfathomable mines
> Of never-failing skill
> He treasures up His bright designs
> And works His sovereign will.
>
> His purposes will ripen fast,
> Unfolding every hour;
> The bud may have a bitter taste,
> But sweet will be the flower.
>
> Blind unbelief is sure to err
> And scan His work in vain;
> God is His own interpreter,
> And He will make it plain.[2]

What an incredible expression of worship from a heart assured that we can trust our lives fully to God! Cowper worshiped

Him as the One with all things under His control—that even when he could not fathom God's ways in his life, God was working out His good, pleasing, and perfect will. The hymn declares, "God is His own interpreter." In other words, we cannot always speak for Him or figure Him out. In His own timing, we will begin to perceive the wonders that He is performing.

But the most amazing thing of all about this hymn is that Cowper suffered with manic depression—something that he'd been plagued by for many years and that doctors in his day had little comprehension of. How incredible that he could write such a powerful hymn wrapped around the theme of the sovereignty of God, while living day by day under such a dark cloud! In fact, the day after writing this hymn, Cowper sunk into a deep depression—and for the rest of his days on the earth, he never really recovered. That, in itself, is a mystery.

Yes, there are some things we will never understand while we walk upon this earth. There comes a time when we simply have to submit to the mystery. Why do the young sometimes lose their lives so early on? Why can some people who are so good with children never have sons and daughters of their own? Why would a tsunami hit so hard to wipe out hundreds of thousands of lives in an instant? Theologians and philosophers can weigh in with some interesting and, at times, convincing arguments. But for those who are in the midst of such circumstances, these cerebral answers—feed the mind or offer some explanation as they might—may never fully serve to calm the soul. Sometimes, as we stand there in the midst of our pain and confusion, all we can do is submit to the mystery—knowing that He who gives and takes away is infinitely wiser and more loving than we could ever fathom.

And even if our earthly days cannot make sense of some of these experiences, then our days in heaven surely will. To those who are in Christ, ultimately everything will make sense. The writer of Romans describes it like this:

> I consider that our present sufferings are not worth comparing with the glory that will be revealed in us.
>
> Romans 8:18

We stand on the unshakable hope of all that is to come—for our present suffering, as real and as awful as it may be, will be nothing in comparison with the glory that will be revealed in us. As the apostle Paul encourages us:

> Therefore we do not lose heart. Though outwardly we are wasting away, yet inwardly we are being renewed day by day. For our light and momentary troubles are achieving for us an eternal glory that far outweighs them all. So we fix our eyes not on what is seen, but on what is unseen, since what is seen is temporary, but what is unseen is eternal.
>
> 2 Corinthians 4:16–18

Somehow, this pain, which thunders violently in the very cores of our beings, will be but a mere whisper when compared with the radiance and satisfaction to one day be bestowed upon us. It's good news from a distant land, the glimmering haze of a bright hope to come. And yet it is not escapism—for though this hope will be fully unveiled to us on that day, even now we can live in Christ, and He in us. We walk on: sorrowful, yet always rejoicing; perplexed, but never in despair; at times having nothing, and yet possessing everything.

The road to our final destination will indeed be marked with suffering. Jesus is looking for worshipers who will choose Him even in the midst of their pain. A people with a cry of "Blessed be your name" resonating in the depths of their souls. And no matter how painful life becomes, He will surely be worth the struggle.

Questions for Reflection

1. This chapter talks about the sovereignty of God in everything that happens. How can this bring you comfort as you deal with loss in your life?

2. It is clear through Scripture and in our lives that God does not only give us things—He also takes things away from us. But even knowing this, what truths can you stand on that will never be taken away?

3. Funerals are different for Christians because death is not the end. How does the truth of your eternal destiny affect how you face the losses that come in life?

Discussion Guide
for Small Groups

The following discussion guide was prepared to help you study the concepts in this book in more depth. Scripture passages, questions, reflection notes, and short chapter excerpts will be used to help you process not only the information in the book but also the difficult situations that you have encountered in your life and in the lives of those around you. You can use this guide individually, with one other person, or even in a small group of several people.

If you are the leader of a small group and wish to discuss *Finding God in the Hard Times* and the topic of worship in good times and bad, the following basic guidelines may be helpful. First, before your group meets each week, encourage group members to read the chapter you will discuss prior to arriving at the group meeting, and have them write down any questions or thoughts that occurred to them after reading the chapter. Be sure to bring a Bible on the night of your group meeting, and encourage each group member to do the same, if possible.

Once the group is gathered, allow group members a few minutes to share their initial impressions of that week's chapter. Then, at the beginning of your small-group time, read the brief discussion outline aloud or ask someone in the group to read it aloud. When you come across a question or prompt, allow ample time for each person to share his or her answers, stories, and thoughts. Finally, be sure to create a safe atmosphere so that people will feel comfortable in sharing and opening up to others they may not yet know.

Chapter One: *My Heart Will Choose to Say*

In the opening lines of this chapter, Matt and Beth refer to the act of worshiping God in the hard times as a gutsy, difficult, and costly action, but one that will forge us as the people we are when we're before God in worship. Discuss the following questions with the group:

- In what ways can we choose to worship God in our daily lives in the good times and the bad?

- We all experience low times in life. At what point has worship become "a much gutsier decision" in your life? What happened, and how did you respond?

- Why do we constantly need to focus on God when life gets hard? Do you think God appreciates our broken, trusting worship when we're struggling through the lowest times of life?

In times when life seems like a storm—when the winds blow hard, the waves crash, and everything appears to turn upside down—Matt and Beth ask us to consider the following question: "Can we still find our way to the place of praise?" This is not a question to answer aloud; it's a question for all of us to ponder and answer on our own. For each of us, there are times when life is so painful or confusing that we don't know which way to turn, and we can start to feel spiritually carsick.

Consider the following passage from chapter 1 (and read it aloud as a group):

> There may come seasons of pain when we desperately try to cling to what we know to be true about God, and yet we are utterly confused by a hardship we're experiencing. . . . Before long, we find ourselves in a case of spiritual motion sickness—living in the tension of what we think we know to be true, and the deep pain that seems to contradict it.
>
> The key is to reinforce what deep down you know to be true, by adding extra revelation. Spiritually speaking, roll down the window and stick your hand out.

p. 30

- Matt and Beth say that we should roll down the window and stick our hand out, reorient our minds, and remind ourselves of who God is. What does this chapter say we can do to add this bit of extra revelation?

• What other ways, not highlighted in chapter 1, will help us to remember God's goodness and faithfulness?

In chapter 1, two verses from *The Message* version of Lamentations 3 are used to show us one way to remind ourselves of God's goodness and faithfulness. Turn to Lamentations in a different translation of the Bible and read a bit more of the context. Start in Lamentations 3:17 and read through verse 21.

If you're in a small group, take a moment by yourself and meditate on the words in this passage. Pick out some key words or phrases that stand out to you from these few lines and write them down on a piece of paper, in a journal, or in the margins of this book. Before going on, allow each person in the group to share what they thought about the passage and which words or phrases they jotted down as they read.

• Reflect back on what you read in this chapter. What thoughts or points from this chapter are most comforting to you as you think about the hardest times you've had to endure in your life?

• Have one person read Lamentations 3:22–26 aloud to the group. What are the lessons that can be learned from this simple passage? How does this fly in the face of how we tend to deal with issues that arise in our everyday lives?

Read this passage from chapter 1 and discuss it as the group winds down:

> To worship God is to tell Him that we believe Him for who He says He is. Every day we're faced with the choice to acknowledge and proclaim Him as the great and merciful God He declares himself to be, or to deny Him. Intense though it may sound, the truth is this: If we are to deny something good about God, we automatically imply something bad about Him. . . . There is actually no middle ground. He is either the all-powerful, all-loving God His Word declares Him to be or He is not.
>
> pp. 34–35

At the close of your time together, remind each person to read chapter 2 before your next group meeting. Ask someone to end with a prayer, or close in prayer yourself.

Chapter Two: *The Road Marked With Suffering*

In chapter 2, Matt and Beth begin by recalling 9/11 and the weeks following that harrowing day in New York City. They go on to discuss the fact that many of the churches they visited in America didn't seem to have any songs for times of lament such as this. So Matt and Beth set out to write a song that they could sing in the hard times and, really, in any season of life.

Read the following questions aloud and take a few minutes to answer each with the group:

- Do you think that genuine songs of lament are biblical? Why or why not?

- Matt and Beth state that songs of lament are needed in our churches. Do you think songs of lament, or sorrow, are important and healthy for the body of Christ to write and sing together as part of their worship of God? Why or why not?

- Matt and Beth say that if we choose God, give Him everything we have, and follow Him with all our might, He will not disappoint us. Do you agree with this statement? Why or why not? Why do the authors say that God will not disappoint us?

Consider the following from the text of chapter 2:

For those in pain, it's very freeing to realize that we may ask questions in worship. Jesus himself (our blueprint for perfect worship) did so as He suffered the agonies of the cross. The crucified King of Kings uttered words from a Psalm of lament as He hung in agony: "My God, my God, why have you forsaken me?" (Psalm 22:1; Mark 15:33). Cries for help and painful questions are well within the bounds of healthy and biblical worship.

p. 43

In this chapter, Beth writes how she related to the words in Psalm 73 during a difficult time in her life. Distribute Bibles for each group member (if needed) and allow a few minutes for some personal reflection time. Have each person in the group flip through the book of Psalms and choose a chapter, passage, or series of verses that comes from a place of lament, sorrow, or pain. Ask each person to highlight the passage or series of verses that seem to apply best to a situation they have felt in their lives.

After five or six minutes, ask each person in your group to read a passage and briefly share why he or she chose it. If anyone has trouble finding an appropriate passage, have him or her look up and reflect on Psalm 73 or one of the other chapters from Psalms that are discussed in chapter 2 of *Finding God in the Hard Times*.

- As a group, find and read the following Scripture verses aloud to one another: Psalm 3; 13:1–6; 56; 57; 1 Thessalonians 5:16; James 5:10; 1 Peter 1:6–9. What are the common themes in each of these passages? What responses are recommended when we encounter suffering or sorrow of any kind?

- Why do you think faith in God is so important in this age of doubt, uncertainty, and confusion? Why is the concept of mystery so central to why and how we worship God and place our trust in His plan?

Read this final passage from chapter 2 and reflect on it as the group wraps up:

This is a weighty offering of worship—standing before God, vowing to choose Him above the circumstances of this life, to love and follow Him come what may. But those who do so are never left disappointed, for you cannot out-give God.

There will no doubt be many things in this splintered world that we will not understand this side of heaven. And we simply take assurance in the fact that God is all we have, but more than we need. As John Piper writes: "There are seasons of pain and loss and grief and darkness when nothing else is worth asking for but God."

p. 50

At the close of your time together, remind each person to read chapter 3 before your next group meeting. Then ask someone to end with a prayer, or close in prayer yourself.

Chapter Three: *Though There's Pain in the Offering*

Matt and Beth begin this chapter by discussing two themes: (1) No one goes through this world untouched by tragedy, and (2) wholesome worship never minimizes the pain of this world. The authors state that these dual themes exist together even in the midst of singing a song, and that as we worship God, we have to learn to be thankful in the midst of the pain. Take a few moments to reflect on the following questions with your group:

- What do you think it means to be thankful in the midst of the pain? What kinds of things usually get in the way of our feeling truly thankful when we worship?

- Further along in chapter 3, Matt and Beth unpack the idea that while we don't celebrate pain for pain's sake, times of pain and anguish can bring us closer to God and help us grow. Have you seen this to be true in your own life?

- Now unpack the following line with your group: "There are no wasted seasons in the economy of God." What does this mean to you? Do you agree with it? Why or why not?

- The authors discuss the idea of wholesome worship in this chapter. What do you think is the true essence of wholesome worship?

Now read the following excerpt from the text of chapter 3:

In the natural world, the pruning of a rose bush, for example, ensures that excess is removed, and helps concentrate energy in the plant—getting it ready for more fruitfulness. In the same way, God gets involved in our lives, pruning even what is fruitful so that we may blossom more in our walk with Him.

p. 64

To conclude, allow each person a few minutes to skim through chapter 3. Have the group members identify a few key points they especially appreciated when they read the chapter. Ask the group what other key points or lessons about suffering they found in this chapter. Allow the group to share their thoughts together.

Next, have everyone get out their Bibles, flip to Genesis 50:1–21, and read the passage aloud together. Talk a bit about the life of Joseph, the suffering he endured, and the amazing way he reacted to his brothers in verses 19–21. Answer the following questions together:

- How did Joseph respond to his own brothers—who had made his life one of misery and suffering? Why is his example particularly insightful for our discussion in this chapter of this book?

- The author of Hebrews talks about hardship in life as a discipline and as a regular part of being a child of God. How do you feel about treating your personal hardships and struggles not as obstacles to overcome but rather as disciplines to cultivate? How does this relate to our worship experience?

As the group's time winds down, read the following passage from Hebrews 12:4–8 aloud:

In this all-out match against sin, others have suffered far worse than you, to say nothing of what Jesus went through—all that bloodshed! So don't feel sorry for yourselves. Or have you forgotten how good parents treat children, and that God regards you as his children? My dear child, don't shrug off God's discipline, but don't be crushed by it either. It's the child he loves that he disciplines; the child he embraces, he also corrects. God is educating you; that's why you must never drop out. He's treating you as dear children. This trouble you're in isn't punishment; it's *training*, the normal experience of children. Only irresponsible parents leave children to fend for themselves. Would you prefer an irresponsible God? We respect our own parents for training and not spoiling us, so why not embrace God's training so we can truly live?

THE MESSAGE

At the close of your time together, remind each person to read chapter 4 in the book before your next group meeting. Then close in prayer.

Chapter Four: *Turn It Back to Praise*

Chapter 4 represents a shift in the book as Matt and Beth focus their attention on the importance of praising God in times when everything in life seems to be going well. Take a few minutes to open your group time today with any praise reports from the group members, and then discuss the following questions.

- Matt and Beth state that "we can be quick to question God when things go wrong for us but slow to honor Him when things go well." Do you find that this is true in your life? Which seems harder for you: to praise God when things are going well or to praise God when life gets difficult? Why?

- Do you ever think about honoring God throughout your week or throughout your day? What ways have you found to worship and praise God that might be unconventional or unique?

Read the following excerpt from chapter 4:

If we can begin to take regular, small steps into thankfulness, then before long we will pick up our pace and find ourselves taking great big strides of praise. Too often we neglect the small things—for instance, saying grace before a meal. In one way, this is a small thing. Yet if we begin to adopt this discipline, we begin to carve out space two or three times each day to thank God for His provision.

pp. 77–78

- Why do you think thanking God for the small things is so hard sometimes? Why is this kind of praise critically important in our relationship with God and in our worship?

- What kinds of small things come to mind for which you feel you need to thank God right now?

After your discussion, take a few moments to allow each person to read Psalms 103 and 104 to themselves. Ask each of your group members to underline or rewrite some of the lines that stood out to them as significant. Take a few moments to reflect on what you and your group read, and then ask each person in your group to share something aloud from these two chapters—a line or a verse that they felt was poignant or added some insight to the discussion so far. Now discuss the following questions together as a group.

- Why is it important to spend so much time focusing on God's glory and His gifts rather than using prayer as a tool to ask for things?

- In this chapter, Matt and Beth also discuss the idea of praising for yesterday, today, and forever. What does this mean to you personally and collectively as a community of followers of Jesus?

- How has God been there for you yesterday and today? Can you thank Him for the blessings of life that are yet to come?

Ask someone to read aloud the following passage from Psalm 105:1–4 as you close out this session with your group:

> Give praise to the LORD, proclaim his name; make known among the nations what he has done. Sing to him, sing praise to him; tell of all his wonderful acts. Glory in his holy name; let the hearts of those who seek the LORD rejoice. Look to the LORD and his strength; seek his face always.

At the close of your time together, remind each person to read chapter 5 before your next group meeting. Then close in prayer, thanking God for being there yesterday, today, and forever.

Chapter Five: *You Give and Take Away*

In Job 1:21, Job cries out, "The LORD gave and the LORD has taken away, blessed be the name of the LORD" (NASB). Job's words are the inspiration for two lines in Matt and Beth's song "Blessed Be Your Name," and the inspiration for the final chapter of this book. Job is an example of a man who was broken down completely yet still able to praise the name of the Lord.

Have someone in the group read aloud the two letters in chapter 5 about Rachel and Natalie. After you have read these letters, allow anyone who feels able to share a difficult time in his or her own life that led him or her to a place of darkness. After those who want to share have done so, ask the following questions:

- Even though these events and struggles do not make sense to you or might seem confusing, how have you learned to put your faith and hope in God?

- Is there a song, a psalm, or another Bible passage that has helped you through a time of utter darkness?

- How do you relate to the stories of Rachel and Natalie? What do you think about when you hear these stories read aloud and consider the heart pangs of these broken parents?

Ask someone to read Romans 8:18–27 aloud to the group. Allow some time for the group members to discuss these verses and reflect specifically on the hope that they have in God's coming glory. As you stand with each other after sharing your own stories and discussing the questions, have each member read through the following excerpt from chapter 5 in the book.

Allow time after reading the excerpt for each person to jot down his or her thoughts.

> Somehow, this pain, which thunders violently in the very cores of our beings, will be but a mere whisper when compared with the radiance and satisfaction to one day be bestowed upon us. It's good news from a distant land, the glimmering haze of a bright hope to come. And yet it is not escapism—for though this hope will be fully unveiled to us on that day, even now we can live in Christ, and He in us. We walk on: sorrowful, yet always rejoicing; perplexed, but never in despair; at times having nothing, and yet possessing everything.
>
> pp. 91–92

After a time of reflection, allow group members to share their notes, their thoughts, their questions, and even their doubts, if they feel comfortable.

Now turn again to the book of Job. In this story, within the first few opening lines, we find much suffering and hardship visited on one man. It appears to be a truly horrible and depressing story, but Job praises God even after some of the worst of his afflictions, saying, "Blessed be the name of the LORD." As Matt and Beth write, "This resounding line is a challenge for every worshiper." Now consider the following questions as a group.

- Read the first chapter of Job aloud as a group and then take a few moments to talk about Job's resounding statement at the end of the chapter. Can you relate to his attitude? What do these lines imply after all Job had suffered?

- Have you ever contemplated the story of Job and God's purpose through it all? Why do you think God allowed Job to suffer through these trials in the first place?

- Give every person seven to ten minutes to write a hymn, poem, or letter of praise to God. Tell each person that he or she might also include specific or personal notes about situations he or she has faced or is facing in his or her life. Tell each group member that he or she might want to include lines about the good and the bad and praising God through it all. Encourage each person to create something personal and unique.

Now have someone in your group read the following passage as the group time comes to a close.

Therefore we do not lose heart. Though outwardly we are wasting away, yet inwardly we are being renewed day by day. For our light and momentary troubles are achieving for us an eternal glory that far outweighs them all. So we fix our eyes not on what is seen, but on what is unseen, since what is seen is temporary, but what is unseen is eternal.

2 Corinthians 4:16–18

At the close of your time together, pray together, lift up one another, and praise God for His goodness and glory and His amazing plan for our lives in good times and in bad.

Bible References
Contained in This Book

The following is a complete list of all the Bible verses referenced in this book. We hope these verses will propel you to further study, and to worship.

Chapter One

I remember it all—oh, how well I remember—the feeling of hitting the bottom. But there's one other thing I remember, and remembering, I keep a grip on hope: GOD's loyal love couldn't have run out, his merciful love couldn't have dried up. They're created new every morning. How great your faithfulness!

Lamentations 3:20–23 THE MESSAGE

How long, LORD? Will you forget me forever?
How long will you hide your face from me?

How long must I wrestle with my thoughts
　　and day after day have sorrow in my heart?
How long will my enemy triumph over me?

But I trust in your unfailing love;
　　my heart rejoices in your salvation.
I will sing the LORD's praise,
　　for he has been good to me.

Psalm 13:1–2, 5–6

Why, my soul, are you downcast?
　　Why so disturbed within me?
Put your hope in God,
　　for I will yet praise him,
　　my Savior and my God.

Psalm 42:5–6, 11

Chapter Two

If one part suffers, every part suffers with it; if one part is honored, every part rejoices with it.

1 Corinthians 12:26

My God, my God, why have you forsaken me?

Psalm 22:1; Mark 15:34

If we are thrown into the blazing furnace, the God we serve is able to save us from it, and he will rescue us from Your Majesty's hand, O king. But even if he does not, we want

you to know, Your Majesty, that we will not serve your gods
or worship the image of gold you have set up.

Daniel 3:17–18

But as for me, I almost lost my footing.
My feet were slipping, and I was almost gone.
For I envied the proud
when I saw them prosper despite their wickedness.
They seem to live such a painless lives;
their bodies are so healthy and strong.
They don't have troubles like other people;
They're not plagued with problems like everyone
else.

Did I keep my heart pure for nothing?
Did I keep myself innocent for no reason?

I was so foolish and ignorant—
I must have seemed like a senseless animal to you.
Yet I still belong to you;
you hold my right hand.
You guide me with your counsel,
leading me to a glorious destiny.
Whom have I in heaven but you?
I desire you more than anything on earth.
My health may fail, and my spirit may grow weak,
but God remains the strength of my heart;
he is mine forever.

Psalm 73:2–5, 13, 22–26 NLT

Rejoice always, pray continually, give thanks in all circumstances; for this is God's will for you in Christ Jesus.

1 Thessalonians 5:16–18

Sorrowful, yet always rejoicing; poor, yet making many rich; having nothing, and yet possessing everything.

2 Corinthians 6:10

Chapter Three

Give thanks in all circumstances; for this is God's will for you in Christ Jesus.

1 Thessalonians 5:18

Consider it pure joy, my brothers and sisters, whenever you face trials of many kinds, because you know that the testing of your faith produces perseverance. Let perseverance finish its work so that you may be mature and complete, not lacking anything.

James 1:2–4

In all this you greatly rejoice, though now for a little while you may have had to suffer grief in all kinds of trials. These have come so that the proven genuineness of your faith—of greater worth than gold, which perishes even though refined by fire—may result in praise, glory and honor when Jesus Christ is revealed.

1 Peter 1:6–7

That is why, for Christ's sake, I delight in weaknesses, in insults, in hardships, in persecutions, in difficulties. For when I am weak, then I am strong.

2 Corinthians 12:10

Endure hardship as discipline; God is treating you as children. For what children are not disciplined by their father? If you are not disciplined—and everyone undergoes discipline—then you are not legitimate, not true sons and daughters at all.

They disciplined us for a little while as they thought best; but God disciplines us for our good, that we may share in his holiness. No discipline seems pleasant at the time, but painful. Later on, however, it produces a harvest of righteousness and peace for those who have been trained by it.

Hebrews 12:7–8, 10–11

And it was only right that he should make Jesus, through his suffering, a perfect leader, fit to bring them into their salvation.

Hebrews 2:10 NLT

Therefore, there is now no condemnation for those who are in Christ Jesus.

Romans 8:1

You intended to harm me, but God intended it for good to accomplish what is now being done, the saving of many lives.

Genesis 50:20

The second son he named Ephraim and said, "It is because God has made me fruitful in the land of my suffering."

Genesis 41:52

He cuts off every branch in me that bears no fruit, while every branch that does bear fruit he prunes so that it will be even more fruitful.

John 15:2

Chapter Four

Enter his gates with thanksgiving
and his courts with praise;
give thanks to him and praise his name.
Psalm 100:4

I praise You because I am fearfully and wonderfully made;
your works are wonderful,
I know that full well.

Psalm 139:14

Praise the LORD, O my soul,
and forget not all his benefits—
who forgives all your sins
and heals all your diseases,
who redeems your life from the pit
and crowns you with love and compassion,

who satisfies your desires with good things
so that your youth is renewed like the eagle's.

Psalm 103:2–5

Chapter Five

The LORD gave and the LORD has taken away; blessed be the name of the LORD!

Job 1:21 NASB

I consider that our present sufferings are not worth comparing with the glory that will be revealed in us.

Romans 8:18

Therefore we do not lose heart. Though outwardly we are wasting away, yet inwardly we are being renewed day by day. For our light and momentary troubles are achieving for us an eternal glory that far outweighs them all. So we fix our eyes not on what is seen, but on what is unseen. For what is seen is temporary, but what is unseen is eternal.

2 Corinthians 4:16–18

Recommended Reading
on Suffering

Carson, D. A. *How Long, O Lord? Reflections on Suffering and Evil*. Grand Rapids, MI: Baker Book House, 1990.

Greig, Pete. *God on Mute*. Grand Rapids, MI: Baker Books, 2012.

Lewis, C. S. *The Problem of Pain*. San Francisco: Harper-SanFrancisco, 2001.

Yancey, Philip. *Where Is God When It Hurts?* Grand Rapids, MI: Zondervan, 1997.

Notes

Chapter 1: My Heart Will Choose to Say

1. Edward Mote, "The Solid Rock," quoted in *The Celebration Hymnal* (n.p.: Word Music and Integrity Music, 1997), song #526.

2. Anonymous, quoted in David Pytches, *Can Anyone Be a Leader?* (Trowbridge, UK: Eagle Publishing, 2004), 43.

Chapter 2: The Road Marked With Suffering

1. John Newton, "Amazing Grace," quoted in *The Celebration Hymnal* (n.p.: Word Music and Integrity Music, 1997), song # 343.

2. Eugene Peterson, *The Message of David* (London: Marshall Pickering, 1997), n.p.

3. Frederick W. Schmidt Jr., *When Suffering Persists* (Harrisburg, PA: Morehouse Publishing, 2001), 26.

4. Mark Greene, lecture at a songwriters consultation, UK, November 2004.

5. Ibid.

6. Schmidt Jr., *When Suffering Persists*, 28.

7. Tim Hughes, "When the Tears Fall," © 2003 Thankyou Music/ Adm. by worshiptogether.com songs. Excl. UK & Europe, adm. by Kingsway Music: tym@kingsway.co.uk. Used by permission.

8. Laurence Tuttiett, "Father, Let Me Dedicate," 1864. In the original, the first line uses *year* instead of *life*. Public domain.

9. John Piper, *Pierced by the Word* (Sisters, OR: Multnomah, 2003), 40.

Chapter 3: Though There's Pain in the Offering

1. "Mental Health," *World Health Organization*, 2005. http://www.who.int/ mental_health/en/ (accessed May 4, 2005).

2. "Africa Fact Sheet," *UNAIDS*, April 3, 2005. http://www.unaids.org/ EN/media/fact+sheets.asp (accessed May 4, 2005).

3. C. S. Lewis, quoted in Russell Stannard, *Why?: Why Evil? Why Suffering? Why Death?* (Oxford: Lion Publishing, 2003), 82.

4. C. S. Lewis, *The Problem of Pain* (San Francisco: HarperSanFrancisco, 2001).

5. Madame Jeanne Marie de la Mothe Guyon, quoted in *NIV Worship Bible* (Grand Rapids, MI: Zondervan, 2000), 59.

6. Frederick W. Schmidt Jr., *When Suffering Persists* (Harrisburg, PA: Morehouse Publishing, 2001), 23.

7. Oswald Chambers, *My Utmost for His Highest* (New York: Dodd, Mead and Company, 1935), reading for October 11.

Chapter 4: Turn It Back to Praise

1. Alfred Painter, quoted in "Alfred Painter," *Wisdom Quotes*, 2004. http://www. wisdomquotes.com/002828.html (accessed May 11, 2005).

2. Wernet Gitt, *The Wonder of Man*, trans., Jaap Kies and Carl Wieland (Bielefield, Germany: Christliche Literatur-Verbreitung, 1999).

3. Ibid.

4. Ibid.

5. Fanny Crosby, "Near the Cross," quoted in *The Celebration Hymnal* (Word Music and Integrity Music, 1997), song # 319.

6. "Great Is Thy Faithfulness," quoted in *The Celebration Hymnal* (Word Music and Integrity Music, 1997), song # 139.

Chapter 5: You Give and Take Away

1. These letters have been printed with the permission of the writers, Ruth McColl and Kathy Sayre.

2. William Cowper, "God Moves in a Mysterious Way," 1774. Public domain.

About the Authors

Matt and Beth Redman won the Dove Award for the Worship Song of the Year for "Blessed Be Your Name." Together they have also written "Let My Words Be Few," "Facedown," and "You Never Let Go." Having worked as a full-time lead worshiper from the age of nineteen, Matt has traveled to such places as South Africa, India, Australia, and the United Arab Emirates for worship gatherings, as well as worked with movements such as Passion and Soul Survivor. He is the author of *The Unquenchable Worshipper* and *Facedown* and the songs "The Heart of Worship" and "Better Is One Day." Beth is a former evangelist to school students with the Worldwide Message Tribe and former head of Soul Sister, a ministry arm of Soul Survivor that equips young women. She is the author of the books *Soul Sister* and *Beautiful*.

Matt and Beth live in West Sussex, England with and their five children: Maisey, Noah, Rocco, Jackson, and Levi.

Enter the True Heart of Worship

This book is about a certain kind of worshipper.

Unquenchable. Unstoppable. Undignified. Undone.

On a quest to bring glory and pleasure to God, these worshippers will not allow themselves to be distracted or defeated. They long for their hearts, lives, and songs to be the kind of offerings God is looking for. At life's apex or at its lowest ebb, an unquenchable worshipper is one who rests in an underlying trust in God and worships before an audience of One.

Enter the place where your fire for God cannot be washed away. Become an unpredictable, undivided, unquenchable worshipper.

The Unquenchable Worshipper by Matt Redman

◊BETHANYHOUSE

 Find us on Facebook. facebook.com/BHPnonfiction

 Follow us on Twitter. @bethany_house

Stay up-to-date on your favorite books and authors with our free e-newsletters. Sign up today at bethanyhouse.com.

More From
Matt Redman

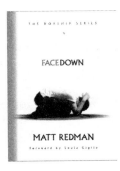

Until we are undone by the knowledge of who God is in all His glory, we will only touch the edges of true worship. When we finally *face up* to the glory of God, we find ourselves *facedown* in reverence and awe. This book will inspire you to embrace this humble posture of the heart—and body—and worship the Almighty in both spirit and truth.

Facedown

Let some of today's most experienced worship leaders guide you into the heart of worship as they explore myriad ways to bring meaningful offerings to the heart of God—thoughts, words, deeds, and songs. For all those who feel called to pursue the depths of worship, this book offers a mixture of creative Bible insights and hands-on advice on how to lead worship and write songs.

The Heart of Worship Files
compiled by Matt Redman

BETHANYHOUSE